HOME PAID, CAR PAID, EVERYTHING PAID

The American Dream

Chapter 1: The Decision to Own a Home

1. **My Journey to Debt-Free Homeownership**
   - Personal story
   - Importance of financial freedom
2. **Making the Decision: Do You Want a Home?**
   - Evaluating the desire and need for homeownership

Chapter 2: Financial Fundamentals

3. **Understanding Amortization**
   - How amortization works
4. **Compound Interest: Friend or Foe?**
   - The power of compound interest

Chapter 3: Building a Strong Financial Foundation

5. **Credit: Your Financial Report Card**
   - Importance of a good credit score
6. **Using 0 Percent Credit Cards Wisely**
   - Benefits and risks

Chapter 4: Smart Spending and Saving

7. **Thrift Shopping and Smart Spending**
   - Saving money through mindful spending
8. **Creating a Savings Fund**
   - Building an emergency fund

Chapter 5: Increasing Your Income

9. **Strategies to Increase Your Income**
   - Side hustles, promotions, and career growth
10. **The Benefits of Earning More Than $60,000**
    - Financial and lifestyle improvements

Chapter 6: The Home Buying Framework

11. **A Framework for Buying Your Home**
    - Steps and considerations
12. **Home Costs and Buyer Beware**
    - Hidden costs and pitfalls

Chapter 7: Financial Tactics

13. **Making Two Extra Payments a Year**
    - Impact on mortgage payoff
14. **Using Math to Your Advantage**
    - Calculations and strategies
15. **Refinance and Fixed Rates**
    - Pros and cons

Chapter 8: Living Below Your Means

16. **Beans and Rice: A Frugal Lifestyle**
    - Budget living tips
17. **How Much You Will Pay**
    - Estimating total costs

Chapter 9: Psychological and Social Strategies

18. **Tell Everyone Your Goal**
    - Building support networks
19. **Faith and Planting a Seed**
    - The power of belief and positivity
20. **Treating It Like a Game**
    - Gamifying your journey

Chapter 10: Pitfalls and Cautions

21. **Buyer Beware: Timeshare and Other Traps**
    - Common financial traps
22. **Don't Play with House Money**
    - Avoiding risky financial behavior

Chapter 11: Tracking and Measuring Progress

23. **Write It Down and Measure Progress**
    - Keeping track of your journey
24. **Realize Where You Are At**
    - Regular financial assessments

Chapter 12: Personal Growth and Success

25. **Building Your Brand and Learning Sales**
    - Personal branding and sales skills
26. **Become a Student of Success**
    - Learning from successful people

Chapter 13: Advanced Strategies

27. **The Inverse Pyramid and Betting the Payment Pyramid**
    - Advanced financial strategies
28. **Taking Advantage of Your Time**
    - Time management and productivity

Chapter 14: Final Thoughts

29. **Using This Book to Achieve Your Goal**
    - Practical application and encouragement
30. **Get Lucky on Purpose**
    - Creating your own luck

CHAPTER 1: THE DECISION TO OWN A HOME

Making The Decision: Do You Want A Home?

Owning a home is often seen as a cornerstone of the American Dream. It symbolizes stability, success, and a place to call your own. However, deciding to buy a home is one of the most significant financial decisions you'll ever make, and it's not one to be taken lightly. I'm going to tell you how I used time on my side to become a homeowner in half the time, 14 years instead of 30. This chapter will guide you through the process of determining whether homeownership is the right choice for you and how homeownership became a reality for me.

A little background, I believe the idea of owning a home started early for me. My parents built their home in the country after living in the big city. Owning that home allowed them to have some stability during economically unstable times, similar to today. My dad was a hardworking man and a preacher in our community Baptist church, but he did not take pay from the church like most. He worked in construction, providing for his five children and wife that way. Mom worked before I was born in daycare and, oddly enough, in a nuclear power plant. However, she was able to stay at home and look after the children when I was growing up.

Even at a young age, I could tell that owning their home gave them a sense of security and accomplishment. My mom and dad would say, "We can sleep at night," meaning that others who paid rent or had a mortgage could not always be sure they could make those payments. I'm sure that thought has crossed many minds, as it did mine for many years. Still, they did it. My parents did not have Master's degrees, nor did they have a lot of money. So, what was the key? Faith, determination, goals, good advice. Yes, all of those played a key role in their success, even when others with more resources could not do it. The lesson is, you have to find what is inside you to make it happen, this goes for anything you want in life. There is a saying that has always stuck in my mind: "He who says he can and he who says he can't are usually both right."

As I said before, some people we knew made twice as much as my mom and dad but still don't own their homes all these many years later, and that was over thirty years ago. The good news is that there are simple things you can do that will change the entire trajectory of your life. Small decisions, small acts of faith, and small differences in attitude and mindset can make you seem lucky, make you feel lucky, and owning a home is one of those.

This book contains over thirty of the most important topics that will contribute to your success, curated from various sources, including family, friends, on-line, co-workers, directors, and my personal experience. I believe the information in this book could literally change your life. In today's world commercial companys are buying up residential property and only renting it out, so home ownership is becoming much more difficult, and more expensive.

The knowledge in this book has taken me over forty years to acquire, connect the dots, and experience for myself. I will walk you through each one and give you the same information I would give to my brothers, sister, nieces, and nephews. I hope this book will be a vehicle to help you reach your goal faster, the same way a car helps you get to your destination faster than walking the same distance.

My parents never made over thirty thousand dollars with five kids. At one point, one child was in college, others in high school, another in elementary school, and a baby at home. My parents taught me many principles and strategies to help me pay off my home in less than half the time. Over time, I learned how to observe and receive lessons from other people and situations that took me from being broke as a joke to a homeowner in fourteen years, home paid, car paid, everything paid!

Thirty years is a long time to finance a home, and the reality that you could pay ninety-nine out of one hundred payments and miss the last one and lose your home, definitely sounds scary. The fact that the landlord can raise the rent, even double it, is equally as scary. Nonetheless, owning a home was a goal for me and my wife. Her family had always rented, and there was a drastic difference in what the word "home" meant to each of us. When I proposed to marry, she started the "engagement to wedding engine." During this time, I felt the pressure to secure a place for us to live. I wanted us to have a home. I guess I wanted us to have that same sense of stability I felt my parents had. If that is what you want, I want the same for you. I want you to enjoy owning your own home. This book not only incorporates how to own your home but valuable life lessons that have made all the challenges and expenses of owning a home worth it. I want you to study this book, read through it, review the chapters, take notes while planning to succeed, and enjoy the journey.

1.1 The Appeal Of Homeownership

The idea of homeownership can be very different from person to person. For many, it represents a milestone of adulthood and financial stability. The idea of having a place where you can paint the walls any color you want, plant a garden, and build memories is incredibly appealing.

However, it's important to separate emotional desires from financial realities. Ask yourself why you want to buy a home. Is it because you genuinely want the stability and control it offers, or are you feeling societal pressure? Understanding your true motivations is the first step in making an informed decision.

1.2 The Financial Reality Of Buying A Home

Before jumping into the home-buying process, you need to take a hard look at your finances. Here are some key considerations:

- **Down Payment:** Do you have enough saved for a down payment? Typically, this ranges from 3% to 20% of the home's purchase price.

- **Monthly Payments:** Can you afford the monthly mortgage payments, including taxes, insurance, and maintenance costs?

- **Emergency Fund:** Will you have an emergency fund left after purchasing your home? It's crucial to have a financial cushion for unexpected expenses.

Create a detailed budget to see how homeownership will fit into your financial picture. If you find that buying a home will stretch your finances too thin, it might be wise to wait until you're in a stronger financial position. Don't underestimate financial creativity. Find ways to increase income and reduce spending. I wouldn't recommend depriving your family of all the great experiences you'd miss by trying to save every dime. I would recommend buying brand new or like new clothes from the Thrift store or cooking at home, it saves a lot of money you can use. I'd recommend a balanced approach that focuses on enjoying your entire journey to homeownership.

Committing is key. You have to know what you want and go and get it. The world is yours. To achieve the goal of homeownership you will have to do what is required to make those monthly payments. I have friends and family that never started paying payments even though they live with family or friends and they still can't afford to. Unfortunately if you don't get yourself to a position where you have to, most usually won't or worse never be able to. I told my wife, "I will find a way, even if I have to work two jobs". When I was younger, I thought that was the type of commitment I needed. The master key here is instead of working two jobs, find out how to earn more. You may be able to accomplish this in your current job. I was never able to, until I started making over sixty-thousand in a company with a well-defined raise structure, yearly raise evaluation period, and COLA (cost of living adjustment).

Learning how to make money quickly is the best way to ensure financial success. Easier said than done, right? Well, actually it is just as easy as it sounds. My best advice is to become a student of success, learn how to make and increase your earnings. If you just take this one piece of advice, you will accomplish your financial goals much, much faster.

If you ask for a job, inquire about pay structure, inquire about what they offer. I worked at a job for six years and got a forty-cent raise over minimum wage. I worked another job across the street and increased my salary by over thirty-thousand dollars in almost the same amount of time, and almost sixty-thousand more than the original job.

The difference between the pay and raises can be drastic from job to job and that difference can affect you and your family's future. Often it is easier to apply for a new job that just pays the salary you want instead of begging a low-paying company for pennies. Find out what jobs pay what you would like to earn. If you are really smart, you'll find out what jobs pay the highest and learn what is needed to do those jobs.

1.3 Renting Vs. Buying

Renting is often viewed as a stepping stone to homeownership, but for many, it can be a long-term solution or trap. Consider the pros and cons of both options:

Renting:

- **Flexibility:** Easier to move for job opportunities or lifestyle changes.(Yep, still under contractual obligation unless they change it in their favor.)

- **Lower Upfront Costs:** No need for a large down payment.(may have wait times and deposits.)

- **Maintenance-Free:** Landlords are typically responsible for repairs and maintenance.(Can't be sure they will fix it when you need it or not raise your rent.)

Buying:

- **Equity Building:** Each mortgage payment builds equity in your home.(In the first years most money goes to interest, more later on this.)
- **Stability:** More predictable housing costs and the ability to personalize your space.(Yep, it costs)
- **Potential Appreciation:** Your home may increase in value over time.(Yep, my home is worth around twice as much)

Reflect on your current life stage, career stability, and future plans. If you anticipate moving within the next few years, renting might be a better option. On the other hand, if you're ready to settle down and want to invest in your future, buying could be the right choice. Home prices rise and fall with economic cycles. Ray Dalio has great videos on economic cycles, how money works, and how credit and debt work. I would advise learning as much as possible from as many reputable action-based content creators you can find. I listen to audiobooks and YouTube daily to keep my mindset focused on success and not distracted by doubt, which is the opposite of faith.

Committing to your goal and taking the steps forward is having faith, and even though you don't know how your success is going to take shape, you still have to move forward. It's called planting a seed. You can plant an apple tree, plant it, nurture it, and it will grow. Treat your journey like you're driving to pick up your first date; have the same excitement, even if you were not familiar with where to go you'll find a way.

1.4 The Impact Of Homeownership On Your Lifestyle

Owning a home can significantly impact your lifestyle. Consider these factors:

- **Responsibility:** Homeownership comes with responsibilities, including maintenance, repairs, and property taxes. (Yea, these suck, prepare for suprises)

- **Time Commitment:** Maintaining a home takes time and effort. Are you prepared to dedicate weekends to yard work or fixing a leaky faucet? (Learn how to fix stuff, It saves lots as most cost is labor)

- **Financial Commitment:** A mortgage is a long-term financial commitment. Ensure you're ready for this ongoing obligation. (Mindset, how can i get this done)

Think about how homeownership aligns with your lifestyle and goals. If you value travel and flexibility, renting might offer the freedom you need. If you desire stability and a place to put down roots, buying a home could be the right path. In the last few years, home prices have more than doubled in a lot of places. Homeownership is becoming much more difficult for the next generation. Companies are buying residential homes and renting them out only! Sometimes these homes are even being purchased sight unseen for triple the purchase price. I'm a firm believer you will find what you are looking for. Don't get into bidding wars or have fear of missing something which could cause you to make bad decisions.

Look around for deals, ask people you know, go and look at homes in person. Let people know you are looking; you never know who may know of your dream home at the price you want. Some homes we looked at were too pricey, some homes were just not nice, clean homes. The realtors tried to convince us that we were lucky when they showed us these run-down "starter-homes". We would barely be able to qualify.

It's sort of a joke now, but at that time it was not funny. In the end, because we were focused on what we wanted and would not take whatever someone else thought we were lucky to have, we got a brand new stick-built home, no one had ever lived in, and they paid us to move in. The company gave us a thousand dollars to move in. I always remember what my dad told me. "Son, if you buy something, make sure you like it, because you are going to be in it, and pay for it."

1.5 Making An Informed Decision

Ultimately, the decision to buy a home should be based on a combination of emotional readiness and financial preparedness. Take your time to research, plan, and reflect on your goals. Talk to trusted friends, family members, and financial advisors to gain different perspectives.

When we bought our home, I would have to borrow twenty dollars to go to work for the next week. But I had just started a new tech job making more money. Taking steps toward my destination made the goal closer. The goal determined what we needed to do, and so we grew to meet the challenge until we met the goal and surpassed the challenge.

Use this chapter as a starting point for your journey. By understanding the emotional and financial implications of homeownership, you can make a decision that's right for you and your future.

In the next chapter, we'll delve into the financial fundamentals of homeownership, including the concepts of amortization and compound interest, which are critical to understanding your mortgage and overall financial health.

CHAPTER 2: FINANCIAL FUNDAMENTALS

Understanding the financial principles underlying homeownership is crucial for making informed decisions and managing your mortgage effectively. In this chapter, we'll explore the concepts of amortization and compound interest, which are essential to grasp as you embark on your journey to pay off your home.

2.1 Understanding Amortization

Amortization refers to the process of gradually paying off a debt over time through regular payments. When you take out a mortgage, your lender structures your loan as an amortizing loan. This means that each payment you make is divided into two parts: interest and principal. I learned about amortization by talking to a coworker about my goals a few years after getting a mortgage.

Interest: The cost of borrowing money, which is calculated as a percentage of the remaining loan balance.

Principal: The portion of the payment that reduces the outstanding loan balance. (paying one extra payment a year can reduce your mortgage by five to seven years)

How Amortization Works

Let's break down how amortization works with a simple example. Suppose you take out a $200,000 mortgage with a 4% interest rate over 30 years. Your monthly payment would be around $955. Each month, part of your payment goes towards interest, and the rest goes towards reducing the principal balance.

Compound interest is known as the eighth wonder of the world for how much money the loaner makes in interest. When considering homeownership, understanding the difference between compound interest and simple interest can be crucial for making informed financial decisions. Here's a breakdown of each type of interest and their implications for homeownership:

Bonus: New money in the economy is created by interest!!

Simple Interest

Calculation: Simple interest is calculated only on the principal amount of the loan. The formula is $I = P \times R \times T$, where:

- I = interest
- P = principal amount
- R = annual interest rate
- T = time (in years)

Implications For Homeownership:

Predictability: Simple interest is straightforward and predictable since it doesn't change over time.

Lower Total Interest: Over the life of a loan, simple interest generally results in less total interest paid compared to compound interest.

Compound Interest

Calculation: Compound interest is calculated on the principal amount and also on the accumulated interest of previous periods. The formula is $A = P \left(1 + \frac{r}{n}\right)^{nt}$, where:

- A = the amount of money accumulated after n years, including interest.
- P = principal amount
- r = annual interest rate
- n = number of times interest is compounded per year
- t = time the money is invested or borrowed for, in years

Implications For Homeownership:

Higher Total Interest: Compound interest results in higher total interest paid over time because the interest is calculated on both the initial principal and the accumulated interest.

Impact of Compounding Frequency: The frequency of compounding (annually, semi-annually, quarterly, monthly, daily) can significantly affect the amount of interest paid. More frequent compounding results in higher interest accumulation.

Practical Example In Homeownership

Consider a $200,000 mortgage with an annual interest rate of 5% over 30 years:

Simple Interest Calculation:

Total Interest = Principal * Rate * Time

Total Interest = $200,000 * 0.05 * 30 = $300,000

Total Amount Paid = Principal + Interest = $200,000 + $300,000 = $500,000

Compound Interest Calculation:

For simplicity, assuming annual compounding:

Total Amount Paid \(A = 200,000 \left(1 + \frac{0.05}{1}\right)^{30} \approx 200,000 \left(4.3219\right) \approx 864,380 \)

Total Interest = Total Amount Paid - Principal = $864,380 - $200,000 = $664,380

Which Is Better For Homeownership?

Simple Interest Loans: These are less common for mortgages but can be advantageous due to lower overall interest costs.

Compound Interest Loans: Most mortgages use compound interest, particularly with monthly compounding. While more expensive, these are more widely available and often come with other benefits, such as fixed rates and longer terms.

Tips For Homeowners

Understand Your Loan Terms: Know whether your mortgage uses simple or compound interest and how frequently it compounds.

Compare Loan Options: Look at total interest costs over the life of the loan, not just monthly payments.

Consider Early Repayment: Paying off a mortgage early can reduce the total interest paid, especially for compound interest loans.

Understanding these concepts can help you make more informed decisions about financing your home and managing your mortgage effectively.

In the early years of your mortgage, a larger portion of your payment goes towards interest because the outstanding loan balance is higher. As you pay down the principal, the interest portion decreases, and more of your payment goes towards the principal. This gradual shift continues until the loan is fully paid off. If you pay off fifty-thousand dollars and you owe sixty thousand dollars your payments still remain the same until you pay the total. I want you to understand, My last payment was thousands of dollars and forty-nine cents and they wanted the nine cents.

The Amortization Schedule

An amortization schedule is a detailed table that shows each monthly payment, the amount applied to interest, the amount applied to principal, and the remaining loan balance. Reviewing your amortization schedule helps you understand how your mortgage payments are structured and how much equity you are building in your home over time.

Here is a simplified example of an amortization schedule for the first few months:

Payment #	Payment Amount	Interest Paid	Principal Paid	Remaining Balance
1	$955	$667	$288	$199,712
2	$955	$666	$289	$199,423
3	$955	$665	$290	$199,133

As you can see, with each payment, the amount going towards the principal increases slightly, while the interest portion decreases.

2.2 Compound Interest: Friend Or Foe?

Compound interest is the interest calculated on the initial principal, which also includes all the accumulated interest from previous periods. It's a powerful concept that can work for you or against you, depending on whether you're earning it or paying for it.

Compound Interest In Savings

When you save or invest money, compound interest helps your money grow faster. For example, if you invest $10,000 at an annual interest rate of 5%, compounded annually, your investment will grow as follows:

- Year 1: $10,000 x 1.05 = $10,500
- Year 2: $10,500 x 1.05 = $11,025
- Year 3: $11,025 x 1.05 = $11,576

After three years, your investment grows to $11,576, thanks to compound interest.

Compound Interest In Mortgages

On the flip side, when you have a loan like a mortgage, compound interest works against you. The interest you pay compounds over time, making it crucial to pay down your principal as quickly as possible to reduce the total interest paid.

The Power Of Extra Payments

One of the most effective ways to combat compound interest in a mortgage is by making extra payments towards the principal.

Even small additional payments can significantly reduce the amount of interest you pay over the life of the loan.

For example, if you make an extra $100 payment towards the principal each month on a 30-year mortgage, you can shorten the loan term and save thousands in interest.

2.3 Practical Tips For Managing Amortization And Compound Interest

- **Review Your Amortization Schedule:** Regularly review your amortization schedule to understand how your payments are applied and to track your progress.

- **Make Extra Payments:** Whenever possible, make extra payments towards the principal to reduce the total interest paid and shorten the loan term.

- **Consider Bi-Weekly Payments:** Instead of making monthly payments, consider making bi-weekly payments. This results in one extra payment each year, which can significantly reduce the loan term and interest paid.

- **Refinance for a Better Rate:** If interest rates drop or your credit improves, consider refinancing your mortgage to secure a lower interest rate, reducing the amount of interest you'll pay over the life of the loan.

Understanding the principles of amortization and compound interest is fundamental to managing your mortgage effectively. By leveraging these concepts, you can make informed decisions, reduce your interest payments, and pay off your home faster.

In the next chapter, we'll delve into building a strong financial foundation, including the importance of maintaining good credit and using zero percent credit cards wisely.

CHAPTER 3: BUILDING A STRONG FINANCIAL FOUNDATION

To achieve your goal of paying off your home as fast as possible, you need a solid financial foundation. This chapter covers the importance of maintaining good credit, leveraging zero percent credit cards wisely, and other essential financial practices that will set you up for success. You need a credit score of seven-hundred and above. If not you will pay high interest. "Most poor people pay the highest prices". Work on your credit, when I first got married my wife said, "what bills do you have?", at the time I had unpaid student loans and random school related credit card bills, she helped me organize paying them off and after a year or so my credit score was above eight-hundred.

3.1 Credit: Your Financial Report Card

Your credit score is a critical factor in your financial health. It affects your ability to secure loans, the interest rates you receive, and even your eligibility for certain jobs and rental properties. Understanding and maintaining a good credit score is essential for achieving your financial goals.

Understanding Credit Scores

A credit score is a three-digit number that represents your creditworthiness. It is calculated based on several factors:

- **Payment History (35%):** Your record of on-time payments.
- **Amounts Owed (30%):** The total amount of debt you owe.
- **Length of Credit History (15%):** How long you have been using credit.
- **New Credit (10%):** The number of recently opened credit accounts.
- **Types of Credit Used (10%):** The mix of credit accounts you have, such as credit cards, mortgages, and car loans.

Tips For Maintaining A Good Credit Score

- **Pay Bills on Time:** Consistently paying your bills on time is the most significant factor in maintaining a good credit score.

- **Keep Balances Low:** Aim to keep your credit card balances below 30% of your credit limit.

- **Avoid Opening Too Many Accounts at Once:** Opening several new credit accounts in a short period can negatively impact your score.

- **Monitor Your Credit Report:** Regularly check your credit report for errors and dispute any inaccuracies.

3.2 Using Zero Percent Credit Cards Wisely

Zero percent credit cards can be a valuable tool for managing debt and financing large purchases without accruing interest. However, they require careful handling to avoid potential pitfalls.

Benefits of Zero Percent Credit Cards

- **Interest-Free Period:** These cards offer an introductory period (usually 6-18 months) with no interest on purchases or balance transfers.

- **Debt Consolidation:** You can transfer high-interest debt to a zero percent card to save on interest and pay down the principal faster.

Risks of 0 Percent Credit Cards

- **High Interest After Intro Period:** Once the introductory period ends, the interest rate can skyrocket. Ensure you can pay off the balance before this happens.

- **Balance Transfer Fees:** Many cards charge a fee (typically 3-5%) for balance transfers. Calculate if the interest savings outweigh the transfer fee.

Strategies For Using Zero Percent Credit Cards

- **Create a Repayment Plan:** Before taking advantage of a zero percent offer, create a plan to pay off the balance within the interest-free period.

- **Avoid New Purchases:** Focus on paying down the transferred balance rather than adding new charges.

- **Read the Fine Print:** Understand the terms and conditions, including the length of the interest-free period and any fees associated with the card.

3.3 Building And Maintaining An Emergency Fund

An emergency fund is a financial safety net that covers unexpected expenses, such as medical bills, car repairs, or job loss. Having an emergency fund prevents you from relying on credit cards or loans during a crisis, helping you stay on track with your financial goals.

How Much to Save

Financial experts recommend saving three to six months' worth of living expenses. The exact amount depends on your personal circumstances, such as job stability, income, and family size. I started with twenty-five dollars until I reached fifteen-hundred. I told my wife about it and she found a use for it in five days. It took me a year to save that. Later I asked or said "Why did you spend all my stash" she said "You let me." I said "Never again." The money was spent on worthwhile efforts but I realized I needed to protect my stash. Treat your stash like a bank paying back what you use, trust me, just trust me on this one.

I went to my mom and said "I can't save money", she said,"You can save money". I said "I can't" she said "you can!" I submitted to her wisdom and started building my stash back until I had twenty-thousand dollars in an account nobody knew about. I did not count it. Maybe a little a first but, this is real. It was unbelievable to me also. I went to my wife one day and said, "What if we just pay off the house?" she said "what are you talking about?" I said "I have twenty-thousand extra dollars", and within a month the house was paid, car was paid, everything paid. My emergency fund grew to being a house paid fund, that's how important this is. There is much more on this later.

Tips for Building an Emergency Fund

- **Set a Savings Goal:** Determine how much you need to save and create a plan to reach that goal.

- **Automate Savings:** Set up automatic transfers from your checking account to your savings account to build your fund consistently.

- **Cut Unnecessary Expenses:** Review your budget and identify areas where you can reduce spending to contribute more to your emergency fund.

- **Use Windfalls Wisely:** Direct any unexpected income, such as tax refunds or bonuses, to your emergency fund.

3.4 Smart Spending And Budgeting

Living below your means and sticking to a budget are fundamental to financial success. Smart spending and effective budgeting help you manage your money, avoid debt, and save for your goals. We are still working on this one. Remember, you don't have to be perfect to reach yor goal.

Creating a Budget

A budget is a plan for how you will spend your money each month. Here are the steps to create a budget:

- **Track Your Income and Expenses:** List all sources of income and categorize your expenses (housing, utilities, groceries, transportation, etc.).

- **Set Financial Goals:** Identify short-term and long-term goals, such as paying off debt, saving for a down payment, or building an emergency fund.

- **Allocate Funds:** Assign a portion of your income to

each expense category, prioritizing essential expenses and financial goals.

- **Review and Adjust:** Regularly review your budget and adjust as needed to stay on track.

Smart Spending Tips

- **Prioritize Needs Over Wants:** Focus on essential expenses and avoid unnecessary purchases.

- **Shop Smart:** Look for discounts, use coupons, and compare prices to save money on everyday purchases.

- **Avoid Impulse Buys:** Take time to consider purchases and avoid buying items on a whim.

Building a strong financial foundation is crucial for paying off your home and achieving long-term financial stability. By maintaining good credit, using zero percent credit cards wisely, and practicing smart spending and budgeting, you can create a solid foundation for your financial journey.

In the next chapter, we'll explore strategies for increasing your income, including side hustles and career advancements, to accelerate your path to paying off your home.

CHAPTER 4: SMART SPENDING AND SAVING

To achieve the goal of paying off your home fast, it's crucial to not only increase your income but also to optimize your spending and saving habits. In this chapter, we'll explore strategies for smart spending and effective saving, which include leveraging thrift shopping, establishing a savings fund, and fostering a frugal mindset.

Learning how to increase your income through sales and marketing, and pursuing higher-paying opportunities is essential. Start now, time will pass regardless, so use it wisely on your side to pursue financial success. Imagine a ship without a course; it drifts aimlessly. Now, picture a ship with a well-charted destination. Which would you choose to secure your financial future?

4.1 Thrift Shopping And Smart Spending

One of the most effective ways to save money is through smart spending. This means making intentional purchasing decisions and seeking out cost-effective alternatives. One of my biggest secrets is that most of my shirts cost two dollars. I found out at the end of the season some stores took most of their new stock to thrift stores, Goodwill and secondary buyers. Wealthier Individuals would have new and never worn shirts and pants. I could get a weeks worth of shirts for the cost of one shirt in even the cheapest retail store.

The Benefits of Thrift Shopping

Thrift shopping, or buying secondhand items, can significantly reduce your expenses. I mentioned this to a neighbor some time ago and years later he came back to me and said he was able to have better work clothes for himself and dress his children nicer and for a cheaper price than he would paying full price. You have to respect your own money and find ways to maximize it when you have big goals like paying off your home as quickly as possible. Today I don't have to shop in thrift stores, but I do quite often.

Here are some benefits:

- **Cost Savings:** Thrift stores often offer goods at a fraction of the original price.

- **Unique Finds:** You can discover unique, vintage, or rare items not available in regular stores.

- **Sustainability:** Buying secondhand reduces waste and supports environmental sustainability.

Tips for Successful Thrift Shopping

- **Know What You Need:** Make a list of items you're looking for to avoid unnecessary purchases.

- **Inspect Items Carefully:** Check for any damage or wear and ensure the item is in good condition.

- **Visit Regularly:** Thrift store inventories change frequently, so visit often to find the best deals.

- **Be Patient:** It may take time to find what you're looking for, but patience can lead to great bargains.

Smart Spending Practices

- **Price Comparison:** Always compare prices from different stores and online retailers before making a purchase.

- **Use Coupons and Discounts:** Take advantage of coupons, sales, and discount codes to save money on your purchases.

- **Buy in Bulk:** For non-perishable items, buying in bulk can save you money in the long run.

- **Avoid Impulse Purchases:** Stick to your shopping list and avoid buying items on a whim.

4.2 Creating A Savings Fund

Building a savings fund is essential for financial security and achieving your goal of paying off your home. A well-funded savings account provides a safety net for emergencies and helps you manage unexpected expenses without relying on credit.

Types of Savings Funds

- **Emergency Fund:** Covers unexpected expenses like medical bills, car repairs, or job loss. Aim to save three to six months' worth of living expenses.

- **Sinking Fund:** A savings account for planned expenses, such as home repairs, vacations, or large purchases. Regularly contribute a set amount to this fund.

Strategies for Building a Savings Fund

- **Automate Savings:** Set up automatic transfers from your checking account to your savings account to ensure consistent contributions.

- **Cut Unnecessary Expenses:** Review your budget and eliminate non-essential expenses to free up more money for savings.

- **Save Windfalls:** Direct any unexpected income, such as tax refunds, bonuses, or gifts, to your savings fund.

- **Set Clear Goals:** Define your savings goals and track your progress to stay motivated.

High-Yield Savings Accounts

Consider opening a high-yield savings account to maximize your interest earnings. These accounts typically offer higher interest rates than traditional savings accounts, helping your money grow faster.

4.3 Cultivating A Frugal Mindset

A frugal mindset is about being mindful of how you spend and save money. It involves making deliberate choices to live within your means and prioritize financial goals over immediate gratification.

Benefits of a Frugal Lifestyle

- **Financial Freedom:** Living frugally helps you save more money and reduce financial stress.

- **Increased Savings:** By cutting unnecessary expenses, you can contribute more to your savings and pay off debt faster.

- **Environmental Impact:** Frugal living often involves reducing waste and making eco-friendly choices.

Adopting a Frugal Mindset

- **Value Experiences Over Things:** Focus on creating memories and enjoying experiences rather than accumulating material possessions.

- **Embrace Minimalism:** Simplify your life by decluttering and only keeping items that add value to your life.

- **DIY Mentality:** Learn to do things yourself, such as cooking, home repairs, and gardening, to save money.

- **Appreciate What You Have:** Practice gratitude for what you already have and avoid the desire for constant upgrades and new purchases.

Practical Frugal Living Tips

- **Meal Planning:** Plan your meals ahead of time to avoid eating out and reduce food waste.

- **Use Public Transportation:** Save money on gas and parking by using public transportation or carpooling.

- **Buy Generic Brands:** Opt for store-brand products instead of name brands to save money without sacrificing quality.
- **Reduce Utility Bills:** Implement energy-saving practices, such as using LED bulbs, unplugging electronics when not in use, and lowering your thermostat.

Adopting smart spending habits and building a robust savings fund are essential steps towards financial stability and paying off your home. By embracing thrift shopping, creating dedicated savings funds, and cultivating a frugal mindset, you can maximize your financial resources and accelerate your journey to homeownership freedom.

In the next chapter, we'll explore strategies for increasing your income, including side hustles, promotions, and career advancements, to further support your goal of paying off your home in less than half the time like me.

CHAPTER 5: INCREASING YOUR INCOME

Paying off your home in half the time or less requires more than just smart spending and saving; it also involves finding ways to increase your income. In this chapter, we'll explore various strategies to boost your earnings, from side hustles to career advancements, and how you can effectively leverage additional income to pay off your mortgage faster.

5.1 The Benefits Of Increasing Your Income

Increasing your income can provide several benefits:

- **Faster Debt Repayment:** Additional income allows you to make larger or extra payments towards your mortgage, reducing the principal balance faster.

- **Increased Savings:** More income means you can contribute more to your savings and emergency fund.

- **Financial Flexibility:** With a higher income, you have more flexibility to invest, save for future goals, and enjoy a better quality of life.

5.2 Side Hustles And Freelance Work

One of the most accessible ways to increase your income is through side-hustles or freelance work. These opportunities can be pursued alongside your full-time job and can range from leveraging your existing skills to exploring new areas of interest. I created websites and wedding videos. The extra money I would make is only one part, the experience and confidence in my ability lead to an IT job which led to software development and within six year,s a high paying software development career.

Popular Side Hustles

- **Freelancing:** Offer your skills in writing, graphic design, programming, or other areas on platforms like Upwork or Fiverr.

- **Ridesharing and Delivery Services:** Drive for Uber, Lyft, or deliver for services like DoorDash or Postmates.

- **Tutoring:** Provide tutoring services in subjects you excel in, either in person or online.

- **Online Selling:** Sell handmade crafts, vintage items, or unused belongings on platforms like Etsy or eBay.

- **Pet Sitting and Dog Walking:** Offer pet care services in your local community.

Tips for Success in Side Hustles

- **Choose Wisely:** Select a side hustle that aligns with your skills, interests, and available time.

- **Manage Your Time:** Balance your side hustle with your full-time job and personal life to avoid burnout.

- **Set Goals:** Define clear financial goals for your side hustle earnings and track your progress.

- **Network:** Build connections within your chosen side hustle community to find more opportunities and support.

5.3 Advancing In Your Career

Your primary job is likely your most significant source of income, so advancing in your career can substantially boost your earnings. Focus on gaining skills, seeking promotions, and negotiating your salary to maximize your income potential.

Gaining New Skills

- **Continuing Education:** Take courses or earn certifications in your field to enhance your qualifications and make you more competitive.

- **Professional Development:** Attend workshops, seminars, and conferences to stay updated on industry trends and network with professionals.

- **Soft Skills:** Develop essential soft skills like communication, leadership, and time management, which are valuable in any career.

Seeking Promotions

- **Exceed Expectations:** Consistently perform at a high level and take on additional responsibilities to demonstrate your value.

- **Build Relationships:** Cultivate positive relationships with colleagues, supervisors, and mentors who can support your career advancement.

- **Communicate Goals:** Express your career goals to your manager and seek feedback on how to achieve them.

Salary Negotiation

- **Research:** Understand the market rate for your role and experience level to inform your negotiation.

- **Highlight Achievements:** Clearly articulate your accomplishments and the value you bring to the company.

- **Be Confident:** Approach the negotiation with confidence and be prepared to discuss your salary expectations.

5.4 Passive Income Streams

Passive income streams require upfront effort but can provide ongoing earnings with minimal maintenance. These income sources can complement your active income and accelerate your mortgage payoff.

Types of Passive Income

- **Investments:** Invest in stocks, bonds, or real estate to generate dividends, interest, or rental income.

- **Rental Property:** Purchase property to rent out, creating a steady stream of rental income.

- **Digital Products:** Create and sell digital products like eBooks, online courses, or software.
- **Peer-to-Peer Lending:** Lend money through peer-to-peer lending platforms and earn interest on the loans.

Building Passive Income Streams

- **Start Small:** Begin with one passive income stream and gradually expand as you gain experience and confidence.

- **Diversify:** Spread your investments across different income streams to reduce risk.

- **Reinvest Earnings:** Reinvest the income generated from passive sources to grow your earnings over time.

5.5 Leveraging Additional Income To Pay Off Your Mortgage

Once you've increased your income, it's essential to use it effectively to pay off your mortgage faster.

Make Extra Payments

Use your additional income to make extra payments towards your mortgage principal. Even small additional payments can significantly reduce the interest you pay over the life of the loan. We started with one extra payment a year and that took us a few years to get there.

Refinance for Better Terms

If interest rates drop or your credit improves, consider refinancing your mortgage to secure a lower interest rate or a shorter loan term. This can reduce your monthly payments and overall interest, freeing up more income to pay down the principal. Learning about economic cycles really helped me see future possibilities and make better decisions.

Allocate Windfalls

Direct any windfalls, such as tax refunds, bonuses, or gifts, towards your mortgage. These lump-sum payments can make a significant dent in your principal balance.

Stay Disciplined

Maintain a disciplined approach to using your additional income for mortgage payments. Avoid lifestyle inflation and prioritize paying off your home over unnecessary spending.

Increasing your income is a powerful strategy for achieving your goal of paying off your home. Whether through side hustles, career advancements, or passive income streams, additional earnings can accelerate your mortgage payoff and enhance your financial stability.

In the next chapter, we'll discuss the importance of setting clear financial goals, creating a detailed plan, and tracking your progress to stay motivated and on track towards paying off your home.

CHAPTER 6: THE HOME BUYING FRAMEWORK

Buying a home is a significant financial decision that requires careful planning and consideration. In this chapter, we'll explore the essential steps and considerations in the home buying process, from assessing your readiness to navigating the complexities of mortgage options and property selection.

6.1 Assessing Your Readiness

Before diving into the home buying process, it's crucial to assess your financial readiness and determine if now is the right time to buy a home.

Financial Readiness

- **Credit Score:** Check your credit score and address any issues or discrepancies that may impact your ability to secure a mortgage.

- **Debt-to-Income Ratio:** Calculate your debt-to-income ratio to understand how much of your income goes towards debt payments.

- **Savings:** Ensure you have enough savings for a down payment, closing costs, and an emergency fund.

Personal Readiness

- **Long-Term Plans:** Consider your long-term plans and how buying a home fits into your lifestyle and goals.

- **Stability:** Evaluate your job stability, income potential, and potential life changes that may affect your ability to maintain homeownership.,

6.2 Mortgage Options And Pre-Approval

Understanding your mortgage options and obtaining pre-approval are crucial steps in the home buying process.

Mortgage Types

- **Fixed-Rate Mortgage:** Offers a stable interest rate and consistent monthly payments over the life of the loan.

- **Adjustable-Rate Mortgage (ARM):** Initial lower interest rate that adjusts periodically based on market conditions. (I don't like these as much, unperdictable)

- **FHA, VA, or USDA Loans:** Government-backed loan programs with varying eligibility criteria and benefits. (We got an FHA loan (first time homeowner))

Pre-Approval Process

- **Gather Documents:** Prepare financial documents such as pay stubs, tax returns, and bank statements.

- **Consult Lenders:** Shop around and compare mortgage offers from different lenders to find the best terms.

- **Get Pre-Approved:** Submit an application for pre-approval to determine the loan amount you qualify for.

6.3 Home Search And Selection

Once you're pre-approved for a mortgage, it's time to start your home search and narrow down your options.

Define Your Criteria

- **Location:** Consider factors such as proximity to work, schools, amenities, and neighborhood safety.
- **Property Type:** Decide between single-family homes, condos, townhouses, or other property types based on your preferences and lifestyle.
- **Features:** List must-have features such as the number of bedrooms and bathrooms, outdoor space, and specific amenities.

Home Viewing

- **Attend Open Houses:** Visit properties that meet your criteria to get a feel for the layout, condition, and overall appeal.
- **Take Notes:** Keep track of each property's pros and cons, including potential renovation or repair costs.

Making an Offer

- **Work with a Realtor:** Enlist the help of a qualified real estate agent to guide you through the offer process.
- **Negotiate Terms:** Negotiate the price, contingencies, and closing timeline with the seller to reach a mutually beneficial agreement.

6.4 The Closing Process

Once your offer is accepted, you'll enter the closing process, which involves finalizing the purchase and transferring ownership.

Home Inspection

- **Schedule Inspection:** Hire a licensed home inspector to assess the property's condition, including structural integrity, plumbing, electrical systems, and more.

- **Review Inspection Report:** Review the inspection report in detail and address any significant issues with the seller.

Appraisal and Financing

- **Appraisal:** The lender will order an appraisal to determine the property's market value and ensure it meets lending standards.

- **Finalize Financing:** Provide any additional documentation required by the lender and complete the mortgage application process.

Closing Day

- **Title Search and Insurance:** Conduct a title search to ensure clear ownership and purchase title insurance for protection.

- **Signing Documents:** Attend the closing meeting to sign legal documents, pay closing costs, and finalize the transaction.

- **Receive Keys:** Once the transaction is complete, you'll receive the keys to your new home and officially become a homeowner.

6.5 Post-Purchase Considerations

After purchasing your home, there are several important considerations to keep in mind.

Home Maintenance

- **Regular Maintenance:** Implement a regular maintenance schedule for tasks such as HVAC servicing, roof inspections, and landscaping.

- **Emergency Repairs:** Be prepared for unexpected repairs and have funds set aside for emergencies.

Financial Management

- **Budgeting:** Update your budget to account for new expenses such as mortgage payments, property taxes, insurance, and maintenance costs.

- **Home Equity:** Monitor your home's equity over time and consider leveraging it for future financial goals.

Navigating the home buying process involves careful planning, research, and decision-making. By assessing your readiness, understanding mortgage options, conducting a thorough home search, and completing the closing process, you can successfully purchase a home that meets your needs and financial goals.

CHAPTER 7: FINANCIAL TACTICS

Achieving financial freedom involves implementing effective financial tactics that accelerate your progress towards paying off debt and building wealth. In this chapter, we'll explore strategies such as making extra mortgage payments, using math to your advantage, and understanding the pros and cons of refinancing to help you gain control over your financial future.

7.1 Making Two Extra Payments A Year

Making two extra payments a year on your mortgage can have a profound impact on your payoff timeline. By making these additional payments, you can reduce the principal balance faster, which in turn reduces the amount of interest you pay over the life of the loan.

Impact on Mortgage Payoff

The impact of making two extra payments annually can significantly shorten the length of your mortgage. For example, on a 30-year mortgage, this strategy can reduce the payoff period by up to 7-8 years, depending on your interest rate and loan amount. This means you'll own your home outright much sooner, freeing up financial resources for other investments or savings.

Case Study: John and Lisa's Journey

John and Lisa decided to make two extra payments a year on their $250,000 mortgage with a 4% interest rate. By doing so, they reduced their mortgage term from 30 years to 22 years and saved over $60,000 in interest payments. This extra financial cushion allowed them to invest in their children's education and build a robust retirement fund.

Using Math to Your Advantage

Understanding the math behind mortgage payments is crucial to making informed financial decisions. By calculating the exact amount of interest saved and the reduction in the loan term, you can see the benefits of making extra payments more clearly.

Calculations and Strategies

1. **Calculate Your Monthly Payment**: Use a mortgage calculator to determine your regular monthly payment.
2. **Determine Bi-Weekly Payment**: Divide your monthly payment by two to find your bi-weekly payment.
3. **Multiply by 26**: Multiply this bi-weekly amount by 26 (the number of bi-weekly periods in a year) to find your total annual payment.
4. **Compare**: Compare this total to your regular 12-month payment to see the difference.

For example, if your monthly mortgage payment is $1,200, your bi-weekly payment would be $600. Over a year, you'd pay $15,600 (26 bi-weekly payments), instead of $14,400 (12 monthly payments), effectively making two extra payments.

Practical Steps

- **Automate Payments**: Set up automatic payments to ensure you consistently make extra payments.

- **Budget for Extra Payments**: Adjust your budget to accommodate the extra payments. This might involve cutting back on non-essential expenses.

- **Track Progress**: Keep a record of your payments and monitor the reduction in your principal balance.

7.2 Refinance And Fixed Rates

Refinancing your mortgage can be a strategic move to lower your interest rate, reduce your monthly payment, or shorten your loan term. However, it's essential to weigh the pros and cons carefully.
Pros and Cons of Refinancing

Pros:

1. **Lower Interest Rates**: Refinancing can secure a lower interest rate, saving you money over the loan's term.
2. **Shorter Loan Term**: Opting for a shorter loan term can reduce the amount of interest paid overall, even though monthly payments may be higher.
3. **Fixed-Rate Stability**: Switching from an adjustable-rate mortgage (ARM) to a fixed-rate mortgage can provide stability, protecting you from interest rate fluctuations.
4. **Access to Equity**: Refinancing can provide access to home equity, which can be used for home improvements, debt consolidation, or other financial needs.

Cons:

1. **Closing Costs**: Refinancing involves closing costs, which can be substantial. It's crucial to calculate whether the long-term savings outweigh these upfront expenses.

2. **Longer Break-Even Period**: If you plan to move within a few years, the savings from refinancing might not cover the closing costs.
   3. **Potential for Higher Payments**: Refinancing to a shorter term can increase monthly payments, which might strain your budget.
   4. **Resetting the Clock**: Refinancing to a new 30-year mortgage can reset the amortization schedule, meaning you start over with more interest payments.

Case Study: Sarah's Refinancing Decision

Sarah had a 30-year mortgage with a 5% interest rate. After 10 years, she decided to refinance to a 15-year mortgage with a 3% interest rate. Although her monthly payments increased slightly, she saved over $80,000 in interest and paid off her mortgage five years earlier than the original term.

Steps to Refinance

   1. **Assess Your Financial Situation**: Ensure you have a stable income, good credit score, and enough equity in your home.
   2. **Shop Around**: Compare rates from multiple lenders to find the best deal.
   3. **Calculate Break-Even Point**: Determine how long it will take to recoup the closing costs with the monthly savings from the lower interest rate.
   4. **Prepare Documentation**: Gather necessary documents, such as income statements, tax returns, and credit reports.
   5. **Close the Loan**: Complete the refinancing process and start making payments on the new loan.

7.3 Using Math To Your Advantage

Math is a powerful tool in managing your finances effectively. By understanding key financial concepts and calculations, you can make informed decisions that maximize your savings and accelerate debt repayment.

Calculations and Strategies

Interest Savings

Understanding how interest works can help you save money and pay off debt faster. By calculating the total interest paid over the life of a loan, you can see the benefits of making extra payments or refinancing.

1. **Simple Interest Formula**: Use the formula $I = P \times r \times t$ to calculate interest, where I is the interest, P is the principal, r is the interest rate, and t is the time period.
2. **Amortization Schedule**: Create an amortization schedule to see how much of each payment goes towards principal and interest.

Compound Interest

Compound interest can work both for and against you. It can grow your investments exponentially or increase your debt significantly if not managed properly.

1. **Compound Interest Formula**: Use the formula $A = P\left(1 + \frac{r}{n}\right)^{nt}$, where A is the amount of money accumulated after n periods, P is the principal, r is the annual interest rate, n is the number of times interest is compounded per year, and t is the number of years.

Budgeting

A well-planned budget is essential for managing your finances and achieving your goals. By tracking your income and expenses, you can identify areas to cut costs and save more money.

1. **50/30/20 Rule**: Allocate 50% of your income to needs, 30% to wants, and 20% to savings and debt repayment.
2. **Zero-Based Budgeting**: Assign every dollar a purpose, ensuring your income minus expenses equals zero.

7.4 Additional Mortgage Payment Strategies

Making extra mortgage payments is not the only tactic to accelerate your mortgage payoff. Here are some additional strategies that can help you achieve financial freedom faster.

Lump-Sum Payments

Occasionally making lump-sum payments towards your principal can significantly reduce your loan balance and the amount of interest paid.

1. **Tax Refunds**: Use tax refunds to make lump-sum payments.
2. **Bonuses**: Apply work bonuses or other unexpected income towards your mortgage.
3. **Inheritance**: Allocate a portion of any inheritance to pay down your mortgage.

Bi-Weekly Payments

Switching to bi-weekly payments can result in making an extra payment each year, reducing your mortgage term and saving on interest.

1. **Set Up Automatic Payments**: Arrange with your lender to make bi-weekly payments.
2. **Monitor Your Account**: Ensure payments are applied correctly to reduce the principal.

Principal-Only Payments

Specify that extra payments are to be applied to the principal balance, rather than future interest.

1. **Contact Your Lender**: Confirm with your lender that additional payments will be applied to the principal.
2. **Keep Records**: Maintain documentation of all payments and ensure they are applied correctly.

Case Study: Mike and Emily's Strategy

Mike and Emily adopted multiple strategies to pay off their $300,000 mortgage in 15 years instead of 30. They made bi-weekly payments, used tax refunds for lump-sum payments, and ensured all extra payments were applied to the principal. As a result, they saved over $100,000 in interest and became debt-free earlier than anticipated.

7.5 Conclusion: Achieving Financial

Freedom

By making two extra payments a year, using math to your advantage, and considering refinancing options, you can significantly impact your mortgage payoff timeline and overall financial health. The key is to understand the math, evaluate the pros and cons, and make informed decisions that align with your long-term financial goals.

Summary

- **Extra Payments**: Making additional payments can reduce your mortgage term and save on interest.

- **Refinancing**: Refinancing can lower your interest rate and monthly payments, but consider the costs and benefits carefully.
- **Mathematical Strategies**: Use financial calculations to understand and optimize your mortgage and investment decisions.

- **Additional Tactics**: Explore lump-sum payments, bi-weekly payments, and principal-only payments to accelerate your mortgage payoff.

Action Steps

1. **Review Your Mortgage**: Assess your current mortgage terms and explore options for making extra payments or refinancing.
2. **Create a Budget**: Implement a budget that allows for additional mortgage payments.
3. **Track Progress**: Monitor your mortgage balance and track the impact of your extra payments.
4. **Seek Professional Advice**: Consult with a financial advisor to explore the best strategies for your situation.

By implementing these financial tactics, you can take control of your mortgage, reduce your debt faster, and move closer to achieving financial freedom.

CHAPTER 8: LIVING BELOW YOUR MEANS

L iving below your means is a powerful financial strategy that can help you pay off debt faster, save more money, and achieve long-term financial stability. In this chapter, we will explore the principles of frugal living, practical tips for budgeting, and how to estimate and manage your total costs effectively.

8.1 Beans And Rice: A Frugal Lifestyle

Adopting a frugal lifestyle involves making intentional choices to minimize expenses and maximize savings. One of the simplest and most effective ways to embrace frugality is by adopting a basic, low-cost diet, often epitomized by the phrase "beans and rice."

Budget Living Tips

Living frugally doesn't mean sacrificing quality of life; it means making mindful choices about how you spend your money. Here are some practical tips to help you live below your means:

Meal Planning and Grocery Shopping

1. **Plan Meals**: Plan your meals for the week based on affordable, nutritious ingredients like beans, rice, vegetables, and seasonal fruits.
2. **Buy in Bulk**: Purchase non-perishable items such as rice, beans, and pasta in bulk to save money.
3. **Shop Sales and Use Coupons**: Look for sales and use coupons to reduce your grocery bill.
4. **Cook at Home**: Prepare meals at home instead of eating out. Home-cooked meals are typically healthier and less expensive.

Housing and Utilities

1. **Downsize Your Home**: Consider living in a smaller, more affordable home or apartment.
2. **Negotiate Rent**: If renting, negotiate your rent or look for more affordable housing options.
3. **Reduce Energy Consumption**: Save on utilities by reducing energy consumption. Use energy-efficient appliances, turn off lights when not in use, and adjust your thermostat to save on heating and cooling costs.

Transportation

1. **Use Public Transportation**: Save money on gas, parking, and car maintenance by using public transportation.
2. **Carpool or Rideshare**: Share rides with friends or colleagues to reduce transportation costs.
3. **Walk or Bike**: Whenever possible, walk or bike to your destination. It's not only cost-effective but also healthy.

Entertainment and Leisure

1. **Enjoy Free Activities**: Look for free or low-cost entertainment options such as community events, parks, and libraries.
2. **Limit Subscriptions**: Cancel or reduce subscriptions to

streaming services, magazines, and other non-essential services.
3. **DIY Projects**: Engage in do-it-yourself projects for home improvements, gifts, and hobbies to save money and learn new skills.

Personal Finance Management

1. **Track Expenses**: Keep a detailed record of your income and expenses to identify areas where you can cut costs.
2. **Set Financial Goals**: Establish short-term and long-term financial goals to stay motivated and focused on saving.
3. **Avoid Impulse Purchases**: Practice mindful spending and avoid impulse purchases by waiting 24 hours before buying non-essential items.

Benefits of a Frugal Lifestyle

Living a frugal lifestyle offers numerous benefits beyond financial savings:

1. **Financial Security**: By spending less and saving more, you build a financial cushion that provides security and peace of mind.
2. **Debt Reduction**: Extra savings can be used to pay off debt faster, reducing the overall interest paid and freeing up more money in the long run.
3. **Simplicity**: A frugal lifestyle often leads to a simpler, less cluttered life, reducing stress and increasing overall happiness.
4. **Environmental Impact**: Consuming less and reusing more can have a positive impact on the environment by reducing waste and conserving resources.

8.2 How Much You Will Pay

Understanding and estimating your total costs is essential for effective budgeting and financial planning. By analyzing your expenses and identifying areas for potential savings, you can make informed decisions and ensure you are living within your means.

Estimating Total Costs

Fixed and Variable Expenses

1. **Fixed Expenses**: These are recurring expenses that remain relatively constant each month, such as rent or mortgage payments, insurance, and utilities.
2. **Variable Expenses**: These expenses fluctuate from month to month, such as groceries, transportation, entertainment, and clothing.

Creating a Budget

1. **List All Income Sources**: Include your salary, side hustles, investments, and any other sources of income.
2. **Track All Expenses**: Use a budgeting app or spreadsheet to track all your expenses for a few months to get an accurate picture of your spending habits.
3. **Categorize Expenses**: Divide your expenses into categories (e.g., housing, food, transportation) to identify where you are spending the most.
4. **Set Spending Limits**: Based on your income and financial goals, set spending limits for each category.

Reducing Total Costs

1. **Eliminate Unnecessary Expenses**: Identify and cut out non-essential expenses, such as dining out, subscriptions, and impulse purchases.
2. **Negotiate Bills**: Contact service providers to negotiate lower rates for utilities, insurance, and other recurring bills.

3. **Use Cashback and Rewards**: Take advantage of cashback offers and rewards programs to save money on everyday purchases.
4. **Buy Used or Refurbished**: Purchase used or refurbished items, such as electronics, furniture, and clothing, to save money.

Practical Examples

1. **Grocery Savings**: By meal planning, buying in bulk, and using coupons, a family of four can save up to $200 per month on groceries.
2. **Energy Savings**: By reducing energy consumption and using energy-efficient appliances, households can save up to 20% on utility bills.
3. **Transportation Savings**: Using public transportation or carpooling can save individuals up to $150 per month on gas and maintenance costs.

Tracking and Adjusting Your Budget

1. **Regular Review**: Review your budget monthly to track your progress and adjust spending limits as needed.
2. **Adjust for Changes**: Be flexible and adjust your budget to account for changes in income, expenses, or financial goals.
3. **Celebrate Milestones**: Acknowledge and celebrate when you reach financial milestones, such as paying off a debt or reaching a savings goal.

Case Study: The Johnson Family

The Johnson family decided to live below their means to save for their children's education and an early retirement. They tracked their expenses, created a budget, and implemented several cost-saving strategies:

- **Grocery Savings**: By meal planning, shopping sales, and cooking at home, they reduced their grocery bill by $150 per month.

- **Energy Savings**: They installed energy-efficient appliances and reduced their energy consumption, saving $50 per month on utilities.

- **Transportation Savings**: They started carpooling and using public transportation, saving $100 per month on gas and maintenance.

By living below their means, the Johnsons saved an additional $300 per month, which they used to pay off debt and build their savings.

8.3 Practical Steps For Living Below Your Means

Implementing a frugal lifestyle requires intentional planning and consistent effort. Here are some practical steps to help you get started:

Step 1: Assess Your Financial Situation

1. **Calculate Net Worth**: Determine your net worth by subtracting your liabilities from your assets.
2. **Identify Financial Goals**: Set clear financial goals, such as paying off debt, building an emergency fund, or saving for a major purchase.

Step 2: Create a Detailed Budget

1. **Track Income and Expenses**: Use a budgeting tool to track all sources of income and expenses.

2. **Categorize Spending**: Divide your expenses into categories and set spending limits for each category.
3. **Allocate Savings**: Ensure a portion of your income is allocated to savings and debt repayment.

Step 3: Implement Cost-Saving Strategies

1. **Cut Unnecessary Expenses**: Identify and eliminate non-essential expenses.
2. **Adopt Frugal Habits**: Embrace cost-saving habits, such as meal planning, using public transportation, and DIY projects.
3. **Negotiate Bills**: Contact service providers to negotiate lower rates for recurring bills.

Step 4: Monitor and Adjust Your Budget

1. **Regular Reviews**: Review your budget monthly to track progress and make necessary adjustments.
2. **Adjust for Changes**: Be flexible and adjust your budget to account for changes in income or expenses.
3. **Celebrate Successes**: Celebrate financial milestones to stay motivated and committed to your goals.

Step 5: Build a Support System

1. **Communicate with Family**: Ensure all family members are on board with the frugal lifestyle and understand its benefits.
2. **Join Frugal Communities**: Engage with online or local communities focused on frugal living for support and inspiration.
3. **Seek Professional Advice**: Consult with a financial advisor for personalized advice and strategies.

8.4 Long-Term Benefits Of Living Below Your

Means

Adopting a frugal lifestyle and living below your means offers long-term benefits that go beyond immediate financial savings:

Financial Independence

Living below your means enables you to save more money, pay off debt faster, and build wealth, leading to financial independence. This financial freedom allows you to make choices based on your values and goals rather than financial constraints.

Reduced Stress

By minimizing financial burdens and building a secure financial foundation, you can reduce stress and anxiety related to money. Knowing you have savings and a plan for the future provides peace of mind and emotional well-being.

Flexibility and Opportunities

A strong financial position offers flexibility and opportunities to pursue your passions, invest in new ventures, or take advantage of unexpected opportunities. It allows you to make choices that align with your values and aspirations.

Positive Impact on Relationships

Living below your means can positively impact your relationships by reducing financial stress and fostering open communication about money. Working together as a family or couple to achieve financial goals can strengthen bonds and create a sense of shared purpose.

Legacy and Generational Wealth

By practicing frugality and financial discipline, you can create a lasting legacy for future generations. Teaching your children and loved ones the principles of frugal living and financial management ensures they have the skills and knowledge to achieve their own financial success.

Conclusion

Living below your means is a powerful and sustainable approach to achieving financial stability and long-term success. By adopting a frugal lifestyle, creating a detailed budget, and implementing cost-saving strategies, you can take control of your finances and build a secure financial future.

Embrace the principles of frugal living, track your expenses, and make mindful choices to reduce costs and increase savings. The long-term benefits of living below your means, including financial independence, reduced stress, and greater flexibility, are well worth the effort.

Remember, living below your means is not about deprivation; it's about making intentional choices that align with your values and goals. By doing so, you can achieve financial freedom, build a strong financial foundation, and create a lasting legacy for future generations.

CHAPTER 9: PSYCHOLOGICAL AND SOCIAL STRATEGIES

Achieving financial goals, such as paying off a mortgage early, requires more than just practical financial tactics; it also involves psychological and social strategies. This chapter explores the power of setting goals, building support networks, maintaining a positive mindset, and gamifying your journey to keep yourself motivated and focused.

9.1 Tell Everyone Your Goal

One of the most effective ways to stay committed to your financial goals is to share them with others. By telling friends, family, and colleagues about your goal to pay off your mortgage early, you create a network of support and accountability.

Building Support Networks

The Power of Accountability

1. **Social Accountability**: When you share your goals with others, you create a sense of accountability. People will ask about your progress, and you'll feel more motivated to stay on track.
2. **Encouragement and Motivation**: Your support network can provide encouragement, celebrate your successes, and offer motivation during challenging times.
3. **Advice and Resources**: Friends and family can share their experiences, offer advice, and provide resources that can help you achieve your goals.

Practical Steps To Build A Support Network

1. **Communicate Clearly**: Be clear and specific about your goals. Explain why paying off your mortgage early is important to you and how you plan to achieve it.
2. **Seek Like-Minded Individuals**: Connect with people who have similar financial goals or who have successfully achieved similar goals. Their experiences and insights can be invaluable.
3. **Join Financial Communities**: Participate in online forums, social media groups, or local meetups focused on personal finance and debt reduction.
4. **Involve Your Family**: Make sure your immediate family is on board with your goals. Their support and cooperation are crucial for success.

Case Study: The Smith Family

The Smith family decided to pay off their mortgage early and shared their goal with their extended family and close friends. By doing so, they received encouragement, advice, and even financial tips that helped them stay on track. Their friends celebrated milestones with them, making the journey more enjoyable and less daunting.

9.2 Faith and Planting a Seed

Belief in your ability to achieve financial freedom is a powerful motivator. Maintaining a positive mindset and visualizing your success can significantly impact your journey.

The Power of Belief and Positivity

Visualization and Affirmations

1. **Visualize Success**: Spend a few minutes each day visualizing yourself achieving your financial goals. Imagine the feeling of paying off your mortgage and the freedom it will bring.
2. **Positive Affirmations**: Use positive affirmations to reinforce your belief in your ability to succeed. Repeat phrases like "I am financially free" or "I am paying off my mortgage early" to yourself daily.

The Role of Faith

1. **Belief in a Higher Power**: For many, faith in a higher power provides strength and motivation. Trust that your efforts will be rewarded and that you are supported in your journey.
2. **Gratitude Practice**: Regularly practicing gratitude can shift your focus from challenges to blessings. Reflect on what you are grateful for and how your efforts are bringing you closer to your goal.

Planting a Seed

1. **Start Small**: Planting a seed means starting with small, manageable actions that grow over time. Begin by

making small extra payments on your mortgage or cutting back on minor expenses.
2. **Consistency**: Just like a seed needs regular watering to grow, your financial efforts require consistency. Regularly review your budget, track your progress, and make adjustments as needed.
3. **Long-Term Perspective**: Understand that achieving financial freedom is a gradual process. Stay patient and keep your focus on the long-term benefits.

Case Study: Jane's Journey

Jane started her journey to financial freedom by making small, extra payments on her mortgage. She visualized her success every day and used positive affirmations to stay motivated. Over time, these small actions accumulated, and she was able to pay off her mortgage five years early.

9.3 Treating It Like A Game

Gamifying your financial journey can make the process more engaging and enjoyable. By turning your financial goals into a game, you can stay motivated, track your progress, and celebrate achievements.

Gamifying Your Journey

Setting Milestones and Rewards

1. **Break Down Goals**: Divide your long-term goal of paying off your mortgage into smaller, manageable milestones.

For example, aim to pay off $10,000 in a year or reduce your loan term by six months.
2. **Create Rewards**: Establish rewards for reaching each milestone. These rewards should be meaningful and motivating but not so extravagant that they derail your financial progress.

Using Financial Apps and Tools

1. **Budgeting Apps**: Use budgeting apps that include gamification elements, such as visual progress trackers, achievements, and challenges.
2. **Debt Reduction Tools**: Some financial apps are specifically designed for debt reduction and can help you track your progress, set goals, and stay motivated.

Competition and Challenges

1. **Friendly Competition**: Engage in friendly competition with friends or family members who have similar financial goals. Compete to see who can save the most or pay off the most debt within a certain timeframe.
2. **Challenges**: Create financial challenges for yourself, such as a no-spend month or a savings challenge. These challenges can add excitement and a sense of accomplishment to your journey.

Case Study: The Johnson Family's Game

The Johnson family turned their goal of paying off their mortgage into a game. They set quarterly milestones and rewarded themselves with small treats, like a family outing or a special meal, for each milestone reached. They also used a financial app to track their progress and stayed motivated by seeing their achievements visualized.

9.4 Overcoming Obstacles And Staying Motivated

Every financial journey encounters obstacles. Staying motivated and overcoming challenges is crucial for long-term success.

Common Obstacles

Financial Setbacks

1. **Unexpected Expenses**: Emergencies, such as medical bills or car repairs, can derail your financial plans. Build an emergency fund to cover unexpected expenses without impacting your mortgage payoff strategy.
2. **Income Fluctuations**: Job loss or reduced income can make it challenging to stay on track. Adjust your budget and find ways to increase your income, such as side hustles or freelance work.

Emotional and Mental Barriers

1. **Burnout**: Staying focused on a long-term goal can lead to burnout. Take breaks, celebrate small wins, and remind yourself of the bigger picture.
2. **Doubt and Fear**: Self-doubt and fear of failure can hinder your progress. Use positive affirmations, visualization, and support networks to maintain a positive mindset.

Strategies for Staying Motivated

1. **Regularly Review Goals**: Frequently review your financial goals and progress. Seeing how far you've come can reignite your motivation.
2. **Stay Flexible**: Be willing to adjust your strategies as needed. Flexibility allows you to navigate obstacles without feeling defeated.
3. **Find Inspiration**: Read success stories, listen to personal finance podcasts, and engage with communities focused on debt reduction and financial freedom.

Case Study: Overcoming Setbacks

The Davis family encountered several setbacks on their journey to paying off their mortgage, including unexpected medical bills and a job loss. By staying flexible, adjusting their budget, and relying on their emergency fund, they managed to stay on track and ultimately achieved their goal.

Conclusion

Psychological and social strategies are essential components of achieving financial freedom. By telling others about your goals, building support networks, maintaining a positive mindset, and treating your financial journey like a game, you can stay motivated and overcome obstacles.

Embrace the power of belief, consistency, and accountability as you work towards paying off your mortgage early. Remember, achieving financial freedom is not just about numbers; it's about mindset, support, and perseverance. With the right strategies and a positive outlook, you can reach your financial goals and enjoy the benefits of a debt-free life.

CHAPTER 10: PITFALLS AND CAUTIONS

Navigating the journey to financial freedom involves not only employing effective strategies but also being aware of potential pitfalls and exercising caution. In this chapter, we'll explore common financial traps, the importance of avoiding risky behavior, and how to protect your hard-earned progress.

10.1 Buyer Beware: Timeshare And Other Traps

Many financial traps are designed to look appealing at first glance but can have long-term negative consequences. Understanding these traps and learning to recognize them is crucial for maintaining financial stability.
The Allure of Timeshares

Understanding Timeshares

Timeshares are properties with shared ownership. Owners have the right to use the property for a specified period each year. While this concept may seem appealing for those who enjoy regular vacations, timeshares often come with hidden costs and complications.

Hidden Costs and Complexities

1. **Maintenance Fees**: Timeshare owners are required to pay annual maintenance fees, which can increase over time.
2. **Resale Challenges**: Selling a timeshare can be difficult and often results in a loss. The resale market is flooded with owners looking to offload their timeshares.
3. **Usage Restrictions**: Timeshares come with strict usage schedules, limiting flexibility in vacation planning.

Alternative Options

1. **Vacation Rentals**: Consider renting vacation properties as needed rather than committing to a timeshare.
2. **Travel Savings**: Allocate a portion of your budget for travel expenses and save up for vacations without the long-term commitment.

Other Common Financial Traps

High-Interest Loans

1. **Payday Loans**: These short-term loans come with exorbitant interest rates and fees, often trapping borrowers in a cycle of debt.
2. **Auto Title Loans**: Borrowers use their vehicle title as collateral for high-interest loans, risking their vehicle if they fail to repay.

Pyramid Schemes and MLMs

1. **Pyramid Schemes**: These illegal schemes rely on recruiting new participants to pay returns to earlier investors, eventually collapsing and causing financial loss.

2. **Multi-Level Marketing (MLM)**: MLM companies often require participants to buy products or recruit others to earn commissions, leading to significant personal financial risk.

Recognizing and Avoiding Traps

1. **Do Your Research**: Thoroughly research any financial product or opportunity before committing. Look for reviews, testimonials, and potential red flags.
2. **Ask Questions**: If something seems too good to be true, it likely is. Ask detailed questions to uncover hidden costs and risks.
3. **Seek Professional Advice**: Consult with financial advisors or trusted professionals before making significant financial decisions.

Case Study: Avoiding the Timeshare Trap

John and Mary were tempted by a timeshare presentation offering luxurious vacation options. However, after researching the hidden costs and resale difficulties, they decided to save for vacations instead. This decision helped them avoid long-term financial burdens.

10.2 Don't Play With House Money

Understanding and managing risk is essential for financial success. Engaging in risky financial behavior can undermine your progress and jeopardize your financial stability.

The Dangers Of Gambling And Speculative Investments

Gambling

1. **Financial Losses**: Gambling can lead to significant financial losses, impacting your ability to save and invest.
2. **Addictive Behavior**: Gambling can become addictive, leading to a cycle of loss and debt.

Speculative Investments

1. **High Risk**: Investments in volatile markets, such as cryptocurrencies or penny stocks, carry a high risk of loss.
2. **Lack of Knowledge**: Investing in unfamiliar markets without proper research and understanding increases the likelihood of poor outcomes.

Safe Investment Strategies

1. **Diversification**: Spread your investments across various asset classes to reduce risk.
2. **Long-Term Perspective**: Focus on long-term growth rather than short-term gains.
3. **Research and Education**: Educate yourself about investment options and seek advice from financial professionals.

Case Study: Avoiding Speculative Investments

Lisa was tempted to invest in a new cryptocurrency promising high returns. After consulting with her financial advisor, she realized the high risk involved and decided to stick with her diversified investment portfolio, ensuring steady growth and minimizing risk.

10.3 The Danger Of Debt

Debt can be a significant obstacle to financial freedom. Understanding the dangers of debt and how to manage it is crucial for maintaining financial health.
Types of Debt

High-Interest Debt

1. **Credit Card Debt**: High-interest rates on credit cards can lead to rapidly increasing balances and financial strain.
2. **Personal Loans**: Unsecured personal loans often come with high-interest rates and fees.

Secured Debt

1. **Mortgage**: While a mortgage is often considered "good debt," it still requires careful management to avoid financial difficulties.
2. **Auto Loans**: Secured by the vehicle, these loans can lead to financial trouble if not managed properly.

Strategies for Managing and Reducing Debt

1. **Debt Snowball Method**: Focus on paying off the smallest debts first, then move on to larger ones, gaining momentum as you go.
2. **Debt Avalanche Method**: Prioritize paying off debts with the highest interest rates first to minimize total interest paid.
3. **Debt Consolidation**: Combine multiple debts into a single loan with a lower interest rate, simplifying payments and potentially reducing costs.

Avoiding Debt Traps

1. **Live Within Your Means**: Avoid taking on new debt by living below your means and budgeting carefully.

2. **Emergency Fund**: Maintain an emergency fund to cover unexpected expenses without resorting to debt.
3. **Credit Counseling**: Seek help from credit counseling services if you're struggling with debt. They can provide guidance and support for managing your finances.

Case Study: Overcoming Debt

Mark accumulated significant credit card debt due to impulsive spending. By using the debt snowball method and creating a strict budget, he was able to pay off his debt within three years and regain financial stability.

10.4 Protecting Your Progress

As you work towards financial freedom, it's important to protect your progress and avoid setbacks. Implementing safeguards and maintaining financial discipline are key to long-term success.
Building an Emergency Fund

Importance of an Emergency Fund

1. **Financial Security**: An emergency fund provides a financial cushion for unexpected expenses, reducing the need to rely on credit.
2. **Peace of Mind**: Knowing you have funds set aside for emergencies can reduce stress and allow you to focus on your financial goals.

How to Build an Emergency Fund

1. **Set a Goal**: Aim to save three to six months' worth of living expenses in your emergency fund.
2. **Automate Savings**: Set up automatic transfers to a dedicated savings account to build your emergency fund consistently.
3. **Start Small**: Begin by saving small amounts regularly and gradually increase your contributions as your

financial situation improves.

Insuring Against Risks

Types of Insurance

1. **Health Insurance**: Protects against high medical costs and ensures access to necessary healthcare.
2. **Homeowners/Renters Insurance**: Covers damage to your home or belongings due to disasters, theft, or accidents.
3. **Life Insurance**: Provides financial support for your dependents in case of your untimely death.
4. **Disability Insurance**: Replaces a portion of your income if you're unable to work due to illness or injury.

Choosing the Right Coverage

1. **Assess Your Needs**: Evaluate your financial situation and risks to determine the appropriate types and amounts of insurance.
2. **Compare Policies**: Shop around and compare insurance policies to find the best coverage at the most affordable rates.
3. **Review Regularly**: Regularly review your insurance policies to ensure they continue to meet your needs as your circumstances change.

Safeguarding Against Fraud and Scams

1. **Protect Personal Information**: Safeguard your personal and financial information to prevent identity theft and fraud.
2. **Be Skeptical**: Be cautious of unsolicited offers and requests for personal information. Verify the legitimacy of any financial opportunities or services.

3. **Monitor Accounts**: Regularly monitor your bank and credit accounts for any unauthorized transactions or suspicious activity.

Case Study: Building an Emergency Fund

Sarah prioritized building an emergency fund after experiencing financial strain due to an unexpected medical expense. By setting up automatic transfers and cutting back on discretionary spending, she built a robust emergency fund within a year, providing her with financial security and peace of mind.

Conclusion

Avoiding financial pitfalls and exercising caution are essential components of achieving and maintaining financial freedom. By recognizing common financial traps, managing debt effectively, and protecting your progress with an emergency fund and appropriate insurance, you can safeguard your financial future.

Stay vigilant and proactive in your financial journey. By combining practical strategies with psychological and social support, you can navigate challenges and achieve your financial goals, ultimately enjoying the benefits of a secure and prosperous life.

CHAPTER 11: TRACKING AND MEASURING PROGRESS

Achieving financial freedom requires diligent tracking and regular assessment of your progress. In this chapter, we'll explore strategies for documenting your journey, conducting financial assessments, and staying motivated. By keeping a detailed record of your efforts and understanding where you stand, you can make informed decisions and stay on course to reach your goals.

11.1 Write It Down And Measure Progress

Documenting your financial journey is essential for staying organized, maintaining focus, and celebrating milestones. Writing down your goals, plans, and achievements helps you visualize your progress and stay motivated.

The Importance of Documentation

Clarity and Focus

1. **Setting Clear Goals**: Writing down your financial goals makes them tangible and helps you create a clear plan to achieve them.
2. **Maintaining Focus**: Regularly reviewing your written goals keeps you focused on your objectives and less likely to get sidetracked by short-term temptations.

Accountability and Motivation

1. **Self-Accountability**: Documenting your progress holds you accountable to yourself and reinforces your commitment to your goals.
2. **Celebrating Milestones**: Recording your achievements allows you to celebrate milestones and recognize your hard work, boosting your motivation.

Methods of Documentation

Journaling

1. **Daily or Weekly Entries**: Keep a journal to record your thoughts, challenges, and successes related to your financial goals.
2. **Reflection**: Use your journal to reflect on your progress, identify areas for improvement, and adjust your strategies as needed.

Spreadsheets and Financial Apps

1. **Budgeting Spreadsheets**: Use spreadsheets to track your income, expenses, and savings. Create categories for different types of expenses and monitor your spending

habits.
   2. **Financial Apps**: Utilize financial apps that offer features like expense tracking, goal setting, and progress visualization.

Visual Aids

   1. **Progress Charts**: Create charts or graphs to visualize your progress. Seeing your debt decrease or savings increase over time can be highly motivating.
   2. **Vision Boards**: Use a vision board to display images and statements that represent your financial goals and aspirations.

Case Study: Sarah's Financial Journal

Sarah decided to keep a financial journal to track her progress towards paying off her mortgage. She wrote daily entries about her financial activities, challenges, and successes. Over time, her journal became a source of motivation and reflection, helping her stay on track and make informed decisions.

11.2 Realize Where You Are At

Conducting regular financial assessments is crucial for understanding your current financial situation and making necessary adjustments. Knowing where you stand allows you to set realistic goals, identify areas for improvement, and stay on course.

Conducting Financial Assessments

Monthly Reviews

   1. **Income and Expenses**: Review your monthly income and expenses to ensure you're living within your means and meeting your savings goals.

2. **Debt Reduction**: Monitor your progress in paying off debt. Track your remaining balances and the interest you've paid.

Quarterly Reviews

1. **Savings and Investments**: Assess your savings and investment accounts quarterly. Ensure your contributions are on track and review your investment performance.
2. **Goal Progress**: Evaluate your progress towards your financial goals every quarter. Adjust your strategies if you're falling behind or if your goals have changed.

Annual Reviews

1. **Net Worth Calculation**: Calculate your net worth annually by subtracting your liabilities from your assets. This gives you a comprehensive view of your financial health.
2. **Budget Adjustments**: Review your budget and make adjustments based on changes in your income, expenses, and financial goals.

Tools for Financial Assessments

Personal Finance Software

1. **Comprehensive Tracking**: Use personal finance software that offers comprehensive tracking of your income, expenses, debt, and investments.
2. **Reports and Analysis**: Take advantage of the software's reporting and analysis features to gain insights into your financial habits and progress.

Financial Advisors

1. **Professional Guidance**: Consider working with a financial advisor for professional guidance and personalized financial planning.

2. **Regular Check-Ins**: Schedule regular check-ins with your advisor to review your progress, discuss any changes in your financial situation, and adjust your plan accordingly.

Case Study: Mike's Quarterly Reviews

Mike conducts quarterly financial reviews to assess his progress towards financial freedom. He uses personal finance software to track his income, expenses, and investments. During each review, he adjusts his budget and strategies based on his progress and any changes in his financial situation.

11.3 Staying Motivated Through Tracking

Maintaining motivation throughout your financial journey is key to achieving long-term success. By tracking your progress and setting short-term milestones, you can stay engaged and driven to reach your goals.

Setting Short-Term Milestones

Breaking Down Goals

1. **Smaller Steps**: Break down your long-term goals into smaller, manageable steps. For example, if your goal is to pay off your mortgage, set milestones for paying off specific amounts within certain timeframes.
2. **Realistic Targets**: Set realistic targets that challenge you but are achievable. This helps maintain motivation and prevents discouragement.

Rewarding Yourself

1. **Meaningful Rewards**: Reward yourself for reaching milestones with meaningful and enjoyable rewards. These can be small treats or activities that you look

forward to.
2. **Positive Reinforcement**: Use rewards as positive reinforcement to keep yourself motivated and focused on your goals.

Visualizing Success

Vision Boards and Goal Charts

1. **Creating a Vision Board**: Use images, quotes, and statements that represent your financial goals to create a vision board. Place it somewhere visible to remind yourself of your aspirations.
2. **Tracking Progress with Charts**: Create goal charts to visually track your progress. Color in sections as you achieve milestones, providing a tangible representation of your achievements.

Daily Affirmations

1. **Positive Statements**: Use daily affirmations to reinforce your commitment to your financial goals. Statements like "I am financially free" or "I am making progress every day" can boost your confidence and motivation.
2. **Consistency**: Repeat your affirmations consistently to build a positive mindset and stay focused on your goals.

Case Study: Emily's Milestone Rewards

Emily set short-term milestones for paying off her student loans. Each time she reached a milestone, she treated herself to a small reward, like a favorite meal or a weekend getaway. These rewards kept her motivated and made the journey more enjoyable.

11.4 Overcoming Challenges

Every financial journey encounters challenges. Learning how to overcome these challenges and stay resilient is essential for maintaining progress and achieving your goals.

Common Challenges

Financial Setbacks

1. **Unexpected Expenses**: Emergencies, such as medical bills or car repairs, can disrupt your financial plans. Prepare for these by maintaining an emergency fund.
2. **Income Changes**: Job loss or reduced income can impact your ability to save and pay off debt. Adjust your budget and explore additional income sources if needed.

Emotional and Mental Barriers

1. **Burnout**: Staying focused on a long-term goal can lead to burnout. Take breaks, celebrate small wins, and remind yourself of the bigger picture.
2. **Doubt and Fear**: Self-doubt and fear of failure can hinder your progress. Use positive affirmations, visualization, and support networks to maintain a positive mindset.

Strategies for Overcoming Challenges

Building Resilience

1. **Adaptability**: Be willing to adapt your strategies as needed. Flexibility allows you to navigate obstacles without feeling defeated.
2. **Support Networks**: Lean on your support networks for encouragement, advice, and motivation during challenging times.

Staying Positive

1. **Focus on Progress**: Concentrate on the progress you've made rather than the setbacks you've encountered. Celebrate your achievements, no matter how small.
2. **Maintain a Growth Mindset**: View challenges as

opportunities for growth and learning. A growth mindset helps you stay motivated and resilient.

Case Study: Overcoming Income Loss

David experienced a significant income loss due to a job layoff. By adjusting his budget, seeking temporary work, and relying on his emergency fund, he managed to stay on track with his financial goals. His resilience and adaptability allowed him to overcome the challenge and continue making progress.
Conclusion

Tracking and measuring your progress are vital components of achieving financial freedom. By documenting your journey, conducting regular financial assessments, setting short-term milestones, and staying resilient, you can navigate challenges and stay motivated.

Embrace the importance of clarity, accountability, and positive reinforcement in your financial journey. By understanding where you are and where you want to go, you can make informed decisions, stay focused, and ultimately achieve your financial goals. Remember, every step you take brings you closer to the financial freedom and security you desire.

CHAPTER 12: PERSONAL GROWTH AND SUCCESS

Achieving financial freedom is not just about managing money; it's also about personal growth and developing the skills necessary for long-term success. In this chapter, we'll explore the importance of building your personal brand, learning sales skills, and becoming a student of success by learning from others. These elements are crucial for achieving and sustaining financial freedom, as they enhance your ability to earn, save, and invest wisely.

12.1 Building Your Brand And Learning Sales

Building a strong personal brand and developing sales skills are essential components of professional and financial success. Your personal brand is how you present yourself to the world, and strong sales skills help you effectively promote your ideas, products, or services.
Understanding Personal Branding

What is Personal Branding?

Personal branding involves creating a consistent image and reputation that reflects your values, skills, and experiences. It's how you present yourself to others and how they perceive you.

1. **Identity and Values**: Define who you are, what you stand for, and what you want to be known for.
2. **Consistency**: Maintain a consistent image across all platforms, including social media, professional networks, and personal interactions.

Steps to Build Your Personal Brand

1. **Self-Assessment**: Identify your strengths, weaknesses, values, and goals. Understand what sets you apart from others.
2. **Online Presence**: Create and maintain professional profiles on platforms like LinkedIn. Share content that reflects your expertise and interests.
3. **Networking**: Connect with professionals in your field. Attend industry events, join professional groups, and participate in online forums.
4. **Content Creation**: Share your knowledge and insights through blogs, articles, videos, or podcasts. This establishes you as an authority in your field.
5. **Continuous Improvement**: Regularly update your skills and knowledge. Stay current with industry trends and innovations.

Developing Sales Skills

The Importance of Sales Skills

Sales skills are crucial not just for sales professionals but for anyone looking to advance their career or business. These skills help you effectively communicate your value, persuade others, and close deals.

1. **Communication**: Clear and persuasive communication

is key to successful selling.
2. **Empathy**: Understanding the needs and concerns of others helps you build trust and offer relevant solutions.
3. **Negotiation**: Effective negotiation skills enable you to reach mutually beneficial agreements.

Key Sales Techniques

1. **Building Relationships**: Focus on building long-term relationships rather than just making a sale. Trust and rapport are essential.
2. **Active Listening**: Listen more than you speak. Understand the needs and desires of your potential customers or clients.
3. **Value Proposition**: Clearly articulate the value and benefits of your product, service, or idea.
4. **Overcoming Objections**: Anticipate and address any concerns or objections. Provide clear and convincing responses.
5. **Closing the Deal**: Know when and how to close a deal effectively. This can involve summarizing benefits, asking for commitment, and handling any last-minute objections.

Case Study: Building a Personal Brand

Jennifer, a financial consultant, decided to build her personal brand to attract more clients. She started by creating a professional LinkedIn profile, regularly sharing articles on financial planning, and participating in industry webinars. Her efforts paid off as she became recognized as an expert in her field, leading to increased client referrals and opportunities.

12.2 Become A Student Of Success

Learning from successful people and adopting their habits and strategies can significantly accelerate your journey to financial freedom. By studying the traits, habits, and practices of successful individuals, you can incorporate these elements into your own life.

Studying Successful People

Traits of Successful Individuals

1. **Discipline**: Successful people often exhibit high levels of discipline and self-control. They stick to their plans and routines, even when it's challenging.
2. **Resilience**: They can bounce back from failures and setbacks. Resilience allows them to learn from their mistakes and keep moving forward.
3. **Vision**: Successful people have a clear vision of what they want to achieve. This vision guides their actions and decisions.
4. **Continuous Learning**: They are lifelong learners, always seeking new knowledge and skills.

Methods of Learning from Others

1. **Reading**: Read books, articles, and biographies of successful people. Learn from their experiences, insights, and advice.
2. **Mentorship**: Find a mentor who has achieved what you aspire to. Learn from their guidance and experience.
3. **Networking**: Surround yourself with successful and like-minded individuals. Attend industry events, join professional groups, and engage in discussions.
4. **Observation**: Observe the habits, behaviors, and strategies of successful people in your field. Identify what makes them successful and emulate those traits.

Adopting Successful Habits

Creating Effective Habits

1. **Goal Setting**: Set clear, achievable goals. Break them

down into smaller, manageable tasks.
2. **Time Management**: Prioritize your tasks and manage your time effectively. Use tools like calendars, planners, and productivity apps.
3. **Mindfulness and Focus**: Practice mindfulness and stay focused on your tasks. Avoid distractions and concentrate on your priorities.
4. **Healthy Lifestyle**: Maintain a healthy lifestyle through regular exercise, proper nutrition, and sufficient rest. A healthy body supports a healthy mind.

Case Study: Emulating Success

Tom aspired to be a successful entrepreneur. He studied the habits and strategies of well-known entrepreneurs like Elon Musk and Warren Buffett. By adopting their discipline, resilience, and continuous learning habits, Tom was able to build a successful business and achieve his financial goals.

12.3 Building Your Network

Having a strong professional network is a vital asset for personal growth and success. Your network can provide support, opportunities, and valuable insights that can help you achieve your financial and professional goals.
Importance of Networking

Expanding Opportunities

1. **Career Advancement**: Networking can lead to job offers, promotions, and career advice.
2. **Business Growth**: Entrepreneurs can find partners, clients, and investors through networking.
3. **Learning and Development**: Networking provides access to knowledge, resources, and expertise.

Support and Encouragement

1. **Emotional Support**: A strong network can provide

encouragement and motivation during challenging times.
2. **Mentorship**: Mentors within your network can offer guidance, advice, and insights based on their experience.

Effective Networking Strategies

Building and Maintaining Relationships

1. **Be Genuine**: Approach networking with genuine interest and authenticity. Build real relationships rather than just collecting contacts.
2. **Offer Value**: Provide value to your network by sharing knowledge, resources, and support. Networking is a two-way street.
3. **Stay Connected**: Regularly stay in touch with your network through meetings, calls, and messages. Show genuine interest in their lives and careers.

Leveraging Social Media

1. **LinkedIn**: Use LinkedIn to connect with professionals in your field, join groups, and participate in discussions.
2. **Twitter**: Follow industry leaders and participate in relevant conversations. Share insights and engage with others.
3. **Professional Groups**: Join online professional groups and forums to expand your network and gain insights.

Case Study: Networking for Success

Lisa, a marketing professional, used networking to advance her career. She attended industry conferences, joined professional groups, and actively engaged on LinkedIn. Through her network, she found a mentor, received valuable career advice, and landed a job at a top marketing firm.

12.4 Continuous Learning and Self-Improvement

Commitment to continuous learning and self-improvement is essential for personal growth and long-term success. Staying updated with industry trends, acquiring new skills, and being open to feedback are crucial for staying competitive and achieving your goals.

Lifelong Learning
Staying Updated

1. **Industry News**: Regularly read industry publications, blogs, and news to stay informed about trends and developments.
2. **Courses and Workshops**: Take advantage of online courses, workshops, and seminars to acquire new skills and knowledge.

Skill Development

1. **Technical Skills**: Continuously update your technical skills relevant to your field.
2. **Soft Skills**: Develop soft skills such as communication, leadership, and emotional intelligence, which are crucial for career advancement.

Seeking Feedback
Importance of Feedback

1. **Self-Awareness**: Feedback helps you understand your strengths and areas for improvement.
2. **Growth**: Constructive feedback provides insights that can guide your personal and professional development.

How to Seek Feedback

1. **Ask for Feedback**: Regularly ask for feedback from colleagues, supervisors, and mentors. Be open to constructive criticism.
2. **Reflect and Act**: Reflect on the feedback received and take action to improve. Implement changes and monitor your progress.

Case Study: Continuous Learning

James, an IT professional, committed to continuous learning. He regularly took online courses, attended industry conferences, and sought feedback from his peers. This dedication to self-improvement helped him stay ahead in his field and achieve several promotions.

Conclusion

Personal growth and success are integral parts of achieving financial freedom. By building a strong personal brand, developing sales skills, learning from successful individuals, expanding your network, and committing to continuous learning, you can enhance your ability to earn, save, and invest wisely.

Embrace these elements as part of your journey to financial freedom. Remember, personal growth is a continuous process, and every step you take brings you closer to achieving your financial and personal goals. Stay focused, stay motivated, and keep learning.

CHAPTER 13: ADVANCED STRATEGIES

As you progress on your journey to financial freedom, exploring advanced strategies can further enhance your efforts and optimize your financial outcomes. In this chapter, we'll delve into advanced financial tactics such as the Inverse Pyramid and Payment Pyramid strategies, as well as the importance of time management and productivity in maximizing your financial success.

13.1 The Inverse Pyramid Strategy

The Inverse Pyramid strategy is a sophisticated approach to managing debt and savings simultaneously, aimed at accelerating debt repayment while building savings and investments.

Understanding the Inverse Pyramid

Debt Repayment Priority

1. **High-Interest Debt**: Focus on paying off high-interest

debts first, such as credit card balances or payday loans. These debts typically accrue the highest interest rates, costing you more in the long run.

Simultaneous Savings

1. **Emergency Fund**: Establish and maintain an emergency fund to cover unexpected expenses. Aim for 3-6 months' worth of living expenses in a liquid savings account.
2. **Retirement Contributions**: Contribute to retirement accounts, such as 401(k)s or IRAs, to take advantage of tax benefits and employer matches.

Case Study: Applying the Inverse Pyramid

John applied the Inverse Pyramid strategy by allocating a portion of his income to paying off his credit card debt aggressively while simultaneously contributing to his emergency fund and retirement accounts. This approach helped him reduce his debt burden while securing his financial future.

13.2 Betting The Payment Pyramid Strategy

The Betting the Payment Pyramid strategy involves strategically allocating payments towards debt repayment and investments based on their respective interest rates and returns.

How Betting the Payment Pyramid Works

Prioritizing Debt and Investments

1. **Interest Rate Comparison**: Compare the interest rates of your debts and potential investment returns.
2. **Higher Returns**: Allocate additional funds towards investments or savings that offer higher returns than the interest rates on your debts.

Case Study: Implementing the Payment Pyramid

Sarah implemented the Payment Pyramid strategy by prioritizing debt payments with higher interest rates, such as her student loans, while investing in stocks and bonds that historically provided higher returns. This strategy enabled her to reduce her debt burden while building wealth through investments.

13.3 Taking Advantage Of Your Time

Time management and productivity play crucial roles in optimizing your financial strategies and achieving your long-term goals.

Importance of Time Management

Maximizing Efficiency

1. **Prioritization**: Identify and prioritize tasks that contribute to your financial goals, such as budgeting, investing research, or skill development.
2. **Time Blocking**: Allocate specific time blocks for important activities, minimizing distractions and enhancing focus.

Enhancing Productivity

Effective Work Habits

1. **Goal Setting**: Set clear, achievable goals with deadlines to stay motivated and focused.
2. **Continuous Learning**: Invest time in acquiring new skills and knowledge that can enhance your earning potential and financial strategies.

Case Study: Optimizing Time for Financial Success

Mark dedicated specific time slots each week to review his investment portfolio, research potential opportunities, and update his financial plan. By effectively managing his time and focusing on high-impact activities, he was able to achieve consistent growth in his investments and savings.

Conclusion

Advanced financial strategies such as the Inverse Pyramid and Payment Pyramid methods, coupled with effective time management and productivity practices, can significantly accelerate your journey to financial freedom. By strategically managing debt, prioritizing investments, and optimizing your time, you can maximize your financial outcomes and achieve your long-term goals.

Embrace these advanced strategies as tools to enhance your financial planning and decision-making. Remember, each strategy requires careful consideration and adaptation to your individual financial situation and goals. Stay proactive, stay informed, and continue striving towards financial independence and success.

CHAPTER 14: FINAL THOUGHTS

As you near the conclusion of this journey towards financial freedom and personal growth, it's essential to reflect on the insights gained and prepare to apply them effectively in your life. This chapter serves as a culmination of your learning and provides practical guidance on utilizing this knowledge to achieve your goals. Home paid, car paid, everything paid.

14.1 Using This Book To Achieve Your Goal

This book has equipped you with a comprehensive toolkit of financial strategies, personal development insights, and practical advice. Now, it's time to put this knowledge into action and propel yourself towards your desired financial outcomes.

Practical Application

Setting Clear Goals

1. **Define Your Goals**: Revisit and refine your financial goals based on the insights gained throughout this book.
2. **Create an Action Plan**: Develop a step-by-step action

plan to achieve each goal, including timelines and milestones.

Implementing Strategies

1. **Financial Strategies**: Choose and implement the financial strategies that align with your goals and financial situation.
2. **Personal Development**: Incorporate personal growth techniques, such as building your personal brand and enhancing your skills.

Monitoring Progress

Tracking Your Journey

1. **Measure Success**: Regularly evaluate your progress towards each goal. Celebrate milestones and adjust strategies as needed.
2. **Financial Assessments**: Conduct periodic financial assessments to ensure alignment with your goals and adapt to changing circumstances.

14.2 Practical Encouragement

Achieving financial freedom requires dedication, perseverance, and resilience. During challenging times, draw strength from the following practical encouragements:

Embracing Challenges

1. **Stay Persistent**: Stay committed to your goals, even when faced with obstacles or setbacks.
2. **Learn from Setbacks**: View setbacks as learning opportunities. Analyze what went wrong and adjust your approach accordingly.

Maintaining Positivity

1. **Positive Mindset**: Cultivate a positive mindset to overcome challenges and stay motivated.
2. **Gratitude**: Practice gratitude for the progress made and the opportunities ahead.

14.3 Creating Your Own Luck

Luck often favors the prepared. By taking proactive steps and implementing the strategies outlined in this book, you can create favorable outcomes and opportunities for yourself.

Seizing Opportunities

1. **Be Open-Minded**: Stay open to new opportunities and possibilities that align with your goals.
2. **Networking**: Leverage your network and actively seek opportunities for growth and advancement.

Taking Action

1. **Bold Decisions**: Make bold decisions when necessary, guided by your financial plan and goals.
2. **Continuous Improvement**: Commit to continuous learning and improvement to stay ahead in your financial journey.

Conclusion

In conclusion, this book serves as a guide and companion on your path to financial freedom, personal growth, and success. Utilize the knowledge, strategies, and practical advice provided to create a lasting impact on your financial well-being and achieve your long-term goals.

As you move forward, remember that achieving financial freedom is a journey, not a destination. Stay proactive, adaptable, and focused on your goals. By applying the principles outlined in this book and maintaining a positive mindset, you can navigate challenges, seize opportunities, and ultimately realize your vision of financial independence and success.

Embrace the journey with confidence and determination. Your future financial success begins with the decisions and actions you take today.

CHAPTER 15: DO IT NOW!

As we conclude this journey towards achieving debt-free homeownership and financial independence, it's essential to reflect on the transformative insights and practical strategies explored throughout this book. From understanding the fundamentals of financial management to implementing advanced strategies for wealth accumulation, each chapter has equipped you with the knowledge and tools necessary to navigate your financial journey effectively. Let's recap the key lessons learned and provide final words of encouragement as you move forward on your path to financial success.

Reflecting on Your Journey

Key Lessons Learned

1. **Financial Fundamentals**: You've gained a deep understanding of essential financial concepts such as amortization, compound interest, and the importance

of maintaining a good credit score. These fundamentals form the bedrock of sound financial decision-making.
2. **Smart Spending and Saving**: Through strategies like thrift shopping, smart spending habits, and building emergency savings, you've learned practical ways to manage your finances responsibly and prepare for unforeseen circumstances.
3. **Increasing Income and Home Buying**: Strategies for increasing your income, whether through side hustles or career advancement, have empowered you to pursue your dream of homeownership strategically.

Applying What You've Learned

Practical Application

1. **Financial Tactics**: Techniques like making extra mortgage payments, leveraging refinancing options, and understanding fixed rates have equipped you to optimize your mortgage payoff and overall financial health.
2. **Living Below Your Means**: Embracing a frugal lifestyle and adhering to budgeting principles are key to managing expenses effectively and achieving long-term financial stability.
3. **Psychological and Social Strategies**: Building a supportive network, maintaining a positive mindset, and treating your financial journey as a game have strengthened your resilience and commitment to your financial goals.

Embracing Challenges and Opportunities

Final Words of Encouragement

1. **Persistence and Resilience**: Embrace challenges as opportunities for growth and learning. Stay persistent

in pursuing your goals, even in the face of setbacks.
2. **Creating Your Own Luck**: By applying the principles and strategies outlined in this book, you have the power to create favorable outcomes and seize opportunities that align with your financial aspirations.

Looking Ahead

Continued Growth and Success

1. **Personal Development**: Commit to ongoing personal growth, whether through building your personal brand, refining sales skills, or learning from successful individuals.
2. **Advanced Strategies**: Explore advanced financial strategies like the Inverse Pyramid and Payment Pyramid methods, coupled with effective time management and productivity practices, to maximize your financial outcomes.

Conclusion

In conclusion, achieving debt-free homeownership is not just about reaching a financial milestone; it's about gaining control over your financial future, enjoying peace of mind, and creating opportunities for yourself and your loved ones. As you move forward, continue to prioritize financial discipline, personal development, and the pursuit of your long-term goals.

Remember, your journey towards financial independence is ongoing. Stay committed to applying what you've learned, adapt to changing circumstances, and remain proactive in shaping your financial destiny. By embracing this journey with determination and resilience, you are paving the way for a future filled with prosperity and fulfillment.

Here's to your continued success and the realization of your dreams! Go get some!

www.ingramcontent.com/pod-product-compliance
Lightning Source LLC
Chambersburg PA
CBHW071942210526
45479CB00002B/777